Oxford and Cambridge Progress Tests English

Year 3

Contents

Practice question	2
Test 1	3
Test 2	23

Practice question

The test is in four parts. Each part starts with a reading passage. Read the passage carefully before answering the questions. You will need to look back at the passage from time to time as you work on the questions.

Mark your answers on the answer sheet. Do not make any marks in this booklet.

Each question has four possible answers, marked **A, B, C, D**.

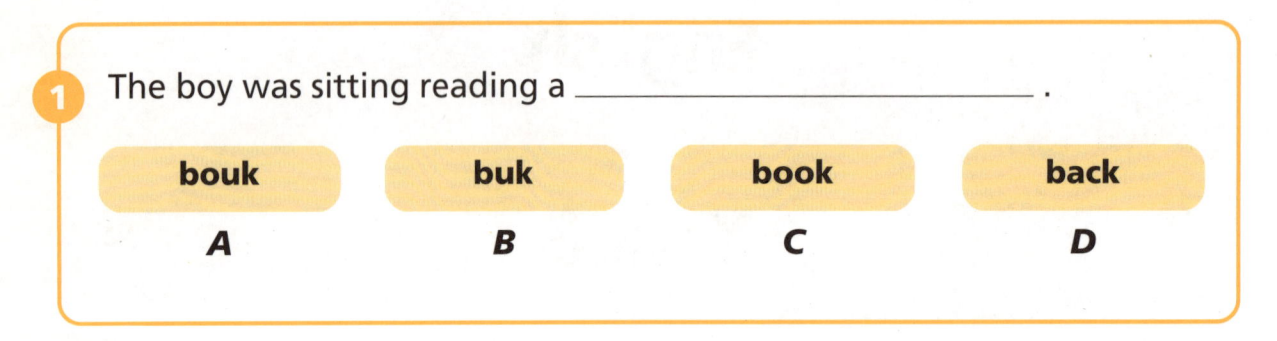

1 The boy was sitting reading a _____ .

bouk	buk	book	back
A	**B**	**C**	**D**

Find the correct question number on the answer sheet and circle the letter to show your answer:

1	A	B	Ⓒ	D
2	A	B	C	D

Try to answer all the questions. Work as quickly as you can, but don't rush.

If you make a mistake, cross out your answer and circle the letter for the correct answer.

2

Test 1

ABOUT CATS

Joanna Troughton

THE TIGER CHILD

The Tiger waited all day for his nephew. When the sun set and the stars came out, he went to the village.

The Tiger Child was tired. He found a house with a warm fire, and fell asleep. The Tiger looked in at the window where the Tiger Child slept.
"You have drunk the fresh milk.
You have eaten the delicious fish.
Now you are asleep by the warm fire.
Tiger Child, you are not a tiger any more...
You are a CAT!"

A domestic kitten

1 When did the Tiger go to the village?

the next morning	straight away
A	B

that night	when the sun was shining
C	D

2 Why did the Tiger go to the village?

to find his nephew	to talk to his sister
A	B

to scare the people	to get some fresh milk
C	D

3 The Tiger Child found a house with a warm fire because he was

hungry.	thirsty.
A	B

scared.	tired.
C	D

4 When the Tiger looked in at the window, the Tiger Child was

sleeping.	drinking milk.
A	B

eating the delicious fish.	looking at the Tiger.
C	D

5 Tigers belong to the same _____ as domestic cats.

A. familie
B. family
C. famely
D. famley

6 Newborn kittens are _____ because their eyes are closed.

A. helpless
B. helples
C. helplese
D. helpeless

7 Cats clean themselves by _____ their fur with their rough tongues.

A. likking
B. licing
C. licking
D. liking

COOKING

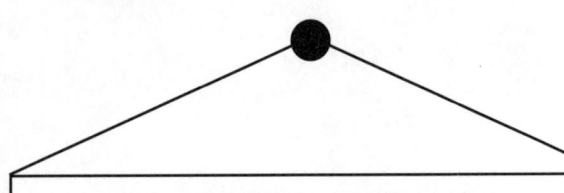

Cooking Rules

Remember these simple rules when you cook.

- Always have a grown-up with you when you cook – it's SAFER that way!
- Always wash your hands and wear an apron. (And NEVER lick your fingers!)
- Always measure carefully.
- Always read the recipe right through before you start.
- Always leave the kitchen clean and tidy.
- Always put your pets out of the kitchen when you are going to cook. They may carry germs which could get into your food.

CHEESE BAKED POTATOES

Ingredients

For 8 people
4 medium-sized potatoes
100g (4oz) grated Cheddar cheese
50g (2oz) butter or margarine
1 tablespoonful milk
1 sliced tomato
salt and pepper

Equipment

baking sheet   fork
teaspoon   small sharp knife
grater   plate
basin   flat serving dish

Method

1. Put oven on at Gas Mark 6 (electricity 200°C).

2. Scrub potatoes well in plenty of cold water. Prick each one with a fork 6 times. Put onto baking sheet.

3. Place in oven for approximately 1 hour until cooked. (*To test*: Push the point of a knife into the centre of the potato; the knife will slide in and out easily when potato is cooked.)

4. When potatoes are cooked, cut in half lengthways. Scoop out centre with a teaspoon, and put into a basin.

5. Add milk, margarine, salt and pepper and three-quarters of the grated cheese. Mix well.

6. Pile potato mixture back into potato shells. Sprinkle remaining cheese on top.

7. Return potatoes to the oven for 20–30 minutes or until cheese melts and browns.

8. Top each potato with a slice of tomato.

9. Place the potatoes onto a serving dish.

Extras

Chopped parsley or ham may also be added when potato mixture is made.

8 The *Cooking Rules* give you

- advice. **A**
- an invitation. **B**
- a reply. **C**
- a story. **D**

9 You should always have a grown-up with you when you cook because

- it's easier. **A**
- it's more fun. **B**
- it's safer. **C**
- it's more difficult. **D**

10 Why should you 'Always put your pets out of the kitchen when you are going to cook'?

- because pets might have germs **A**
- because they might eat the food **B**
- because they might knock things over **C**
- because you might trip over them **D**

11 The recipe gives the correct amounts for

- one person. **A**
- two people. **B**
- four people. **C**
- eight people. **D**

12 How many pieces of equipment are needed?

- 7 — A
- 8 — B
- 9 — C
- 10 — D

13 What does *scrub* mean?

- cook — A
- mix — B
- rub hard — C
- wash — D

14 You know the potatoes are cooked when

- a knife goes into the centre easily. — A
- the skins go brown. — B
- they have been in the oven for one hour. — C
- you prick each one with a fork six times. — D

15 How many ingredients do you have to mix with the potato in the basin?

- 2 — A
- 4 — B
- 5 — C
- 7 — D

16 When do you add the milk to the potato?

　　A　after the slice of tomato

　　B　when the potato has been scooped into the basin

　　C　after 20 minutes

　　D　when you test it

17 *Extras* tells you

　　A　all the other things you could add to cheese baked potatoes.

　　B　everything you must add to cheese baked potatoes.

　　C　some other things you could add to cheese baked potatoes.

　　D　what you must do when the potatoes are finished.

18 There is a box around *Extras*

    A   because some people don't like parsley.

    B   because it's an order.

    C   because you must add ham.

    D   to separate it from the rest of the instructions.

19 Which subheadings tell you what you need to make the potatoes?

Cooking Rules and **Equipment**	**Ingredients** and **Equipment**
A	B
Equipment and **Method**	**Method** and **Extras**
C	D

20 With the use of electrical appliances, preparing food has become much _____ .

easyer	easiyer
A	B
easier	easiere
C	D

21 Prehistoric people _____ learned about cooking by accident.

- **probably** A
- **probablie** B
- **probebly** C
- **probabley** D

22 Holy days, weddings and _____ occasions are often celebrated with a feast.

- **speciel** A
- **special** B
- **spesial** C
- **speshel** D

Andrew Wright

NESSY

Loch Ness is a big lake in Scotland. Some people believe that a monster lives in Loch Ness.

Mr and Mrs Poppleton and Paul Poppleton were on the last day of their summer holidays. They had been touring in Scotland and Paul had insisted that they go to Loch Ness to see if they could see the Loch Ness monster. Mr Poppleton was tired of travelling, he really wanted to get started on the long journey back home.

"There isn't a monster!" he said. "Everyone knows that. All the scientific surveys have shown that the loch is absolutely empty. You've seen enough lochs and one is just the same as the others."

"Oh, let him go and have a look," said Mrs Poppleton, "then we'll have a lovely picnic and set off home. You can have a cup of tea while we are waiting for Paul." So they parked the car by the loch and Mr and Mrs Poppleton settled down to wait for Paul as he set off along the shore. Paul walked along the shore. The day was hot and still; nothing ruffled the surface of the loch, neither a breeze nor a monster. Paul walked quietly, sometimes looking at the loch and sometimes at the stones on the shore. At last he came to an outcrop of rocks. He stopped and wondered whether to climb over them. Then he noticed that one of the rocks was quite different from all the rest; it was smooth and green and sprinkled with red spots.

It was rounded at the sides! He crouched down, and looked at it from below. It was completely round! It wasn't a stone. It couldn't be a stone. It was a huge egg!

23 When did Paul and his parents go on holiday?

spring	summer
A	B

autumn	winter
C	D

24 Paul and his parents went on holiday to

Loch Ness.	Scotland.
A	B

the seaside.	the Lake District.
C	D

25 Paul wanted to look for

Loch Ness.	a monster.
A	B

an egg.	a picnic spot.
C	D

26 Mr Poppleton did not want to go to Loch Ness because

he was afraid of the monster.	he wanted to have a picnic.
A	B

he had seen the monster before.	he wanted to go home straight away.
C	D

27 Paul went for a walk beside the Loch.
What did Mr and Mrs Poppleton do?

- stayed in the car — A
- went for a walk too — B
- had a picnic — C
- started the long journey home — D

28 What was the weather like?

- breezy — A
- hot and still — B
- rainy — C
- calm — D

29 When Paul was walking next to the Loch, he found

- the Loch Ness monster. — A
- a sandy beach. — B
- a rock that was different from all the others. — C
- a boat. — D

30 The egg was

- big and round. — A
- rough and spotty. — B
- small and green. — C
- smooth and made of stone. — D

31 The last sentence of the passage ends with an exclamation mark. This is to show

- A surprise.
- B the end.
- C speech.
- D a question.

32 'It was completely round!' Which word means the same as *completely*?

- A scientific
- B surveys
- C absolutely
- D enough

33 When Paul discovered the egg he felt

- A frightened.
- B excited.
- C sad.
- D angry.

34 Most of the story is leading to

- A Paul and his parents' summer holiday.
- B Paul's walk next to Loch Ness.
- C Mr and Mrs Poppleton.
- D Paul's discovery of a huge egg.

35 Even before people knew about dinosaurs, they told stories about _____ and other fabulous creatures.

dragens	dragones
A	B
dragons	dragerns
C	D

36 Most snakes can move swiftly on land, even _____ they have no legs.

though	thow
A	B
thaugh	theow
C	D

Eileen O'Brien and Diana Riddell

SECRET CODES

Secret codes allow you to send messages, anytime, anywhere. There are lots of different codes that you can use: some are simple, while others may take a long time to learn.

MORSE CODE

Until recently Morse code was one of the most widely-used codes and was well known all over the world. It was invented by Samuel B. Morse and was first demonstrated in 1837. Letters are made up of combinations of dots (short signals) or dashes (long signals). The alphabet is shown below.

A	.–	N	–.	0	–––––
B	–...	O	–––	1	.––––
C	–.–.	P	.––.	2	..–––
D	–..	Q	––.–	3	...––
E	.	R	.–.	4	....–
F	..–.	S	...	5	.....
G	––.	T	–	6	–....
H	....	U	..–	7	––...
I	..	V	...–	8	–––..
J	.–––	W	.––	9	––––.
K	–.–	X	–..–	Full stop	.–.–.–
L	.–..	Y	–.––	Comma	––..––
M	––	Z	––..	Query	..––..

You can send Morse messages in many ways. It's a good idea to repeat your message a few times to make sure it is understood.

Tapping out a message

You can tap out a message on a hard surface, or on a wall between two rooms.

For a dot, make two quick taps.
For a dash make four quick taps.
(Try tapping the letters of your name.)

Between dots and dashes count one.

Between letters count to three.
Count to five between words.

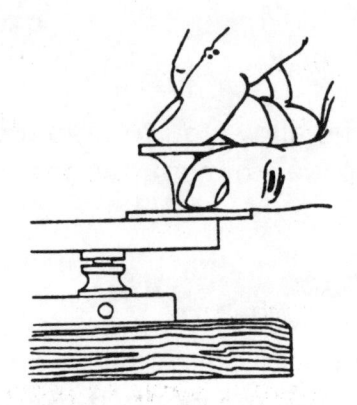

INVISIBLE WRITING

You can also send short, top secret messages that are completely invisible until they are revealed by those cunning enough to know how.

Invisible inks
You can write invisible messages using everyday things. Find out below how to write a message and make it visible again.

Juicy message
To make invisible ink, either grate a raw potato and squeeze the gratings over a saucer, or squeeze half a lemon. Dip a cotton-tipped stick, or a toothpick, into the juice and write your message on pale paper.

Making your message visible
For lemon and potato messages, heat your oven to 120°C, Gas Mark 2. Place the paper on the top shelf for 5–10 minutes, or until the juice has turned brown.

37 How many different secret codes are there?

one	two	a few	many
A	B	C	D

38 Secret codes are

always slow to learn.	difficult to learn.
A	B

easy to learn.	sometimes easy and sometimes difficult to learn.
C	D

39 Samuel B. Morse is famous because he

invented a famous secret code.	invented many secret codes.
A	B

was born in 1837.	was well-known all over the world.
C	D

40 How are messages sent using Morse code?

by Samuel B. Morse	in only one way
A	B

using combinations of letters	using dots and dashes or long and short signals
C	D

41 Why do people repeat the message?

- **A** because it is a good idea
- **B** because they are tapping out a message
- **C** in case they make a mistake
- **D** so they can be sure the message is understood

42 When tapping out a message in Morse code you must

- **A** count three between dots and dashes.
- **B** count to five between different words.
- **C** only make two quick taps.
- **D** tap out the message on paper.

43 The most famous signal sent by Morse code consists of only three letters. It is written like this:

··· ——— ···

What is it?

- **A** etc
- **B** ICI
- **C** SAS
- **D** SOS

44 You can make invisible ink using

- **A** a cotton-tipped stick.
- **B** grated lemon.
- **C** lemon or potato.
- **D** pale paper.

45 'Making your message visible.' *Visible* means

- A it is made of potato.
- B it turns brown.
- C you can heat it.
- D you can see it.

46 The first paragraph is

- A an introduction.
- B an invitation.
- C a conclusion.
- D a summary.

47 What would you need to make an Invisible Writing Kit?

- A cotton-tipped stick, lemon juice, paper
- B ink, paper, pen
- C lemon, paper, potato
- D paper, saucer, toothpick

48 Sign language is a type of code language used by people whose _____ is poor.

- A hearing
- B hereing
- C heareing
- D hareing

49 People with poor _____ read and write using Braille, which is a pattern of bumps on paper.

- A eyesite
- B eisight
- C eyesieght
- D eyesight

50 Unlike sign language and Braille, secret codes were invented to _____ enemies.

- A misleed
- B misslead
- C mislede
- D mislead

Stop – End of test

Test 2

GIANT SNAIL

Giant

There's a giant in our classroom,
He comes from far away,
We've made him warm and
  comfortable,
We're hoping that he'll stay.

He wears a suit of armour
To shield him from attack,
It's hard to tell which part of him
Is front and which is back.

He keeps himself inside himself
Until he moves about,
When eyes and head and everything
Gently ripple out.

His giant foot begins to spread,
His giant eyes explore,
And when he's eaten all there is
He looks around for more.

He waves his giant feelers,
He leaves a giant trail,
I never tire of watching
Our Giant African Snail!

June Crebbin

Hurt No Living Thing

Hurt no living thing;
Ladybird, nor butterfly,
Nor moth with dusty wing,
Nor cricket chirping cheerily,
Nor grasshopper so light of leap,
Nor dancing gnat,
Nor beetle fat,
Nor harmless worms that creep.

Christina Rossetti

1 What creature is the first poem about?

- a giant — A
- a slug — B
- a snail — C
- a tortoise — D

2 This creature comes from

- far away. — A
- inside himself. — B
- somewhere warm and comfortable. — C
- the classroom. — D

3 In the second verse of the poem what does *shield* mean?

- hide — A
- protect — B
- push — C
- pull — D

4 The children look after the snail.
What do the children **not** do to the snail?

- feed him — A
- make him warm and comfortable — B
- play with him — C
- watch him — D

5 Which adjective does the writer use to describe the African snail?

- explore — A
- gently — B
- giant — C
- ripple — D

6 Which word in the poem rhymes with *snail*?

- A African
- B stay
- C trail
- D watching

7 The writer thinks that the creature is

- A boring.
- B frightening.
- C happy.
- D interesting.

8 'It's hard to tell which part of him…'
In the second verse the writer uses the word *It's*. What is it short for?

- A It does
- B It has
- C It is
- D It was

9 '… cricket chirping cheerily'.
Why does the writer use the *ch* in *chirping* and *cheerily*?

- A because it rhymes
- B because the writer thinks it sounds like the noise a cricket makes
- C because *chirping* is a happy word
- D because the writer likes crickets

10 What is the main idea of the second poem?

- **A** There are many different types of creature.
- **B** Some creatures are beautiful and some are not.
- **C** All creatures are important.
- **D** People often hurt little creatures.

11 There are many types of insects that are _____ .

- **A** unown
- **B** unknown
- **C** unknone
- **D** unknowne

12 Butterflies often have _____ wings.

- **A** beuatiful
- **B** buetiful
- **C** beautiful
- **D** beautifull

ANTS

Ants

Ants are a type of insect, that is they have a body that is divided into three parts called the head, the thorax and the abdomen. Ants have three pairs of legs which are all attached to the thorax.

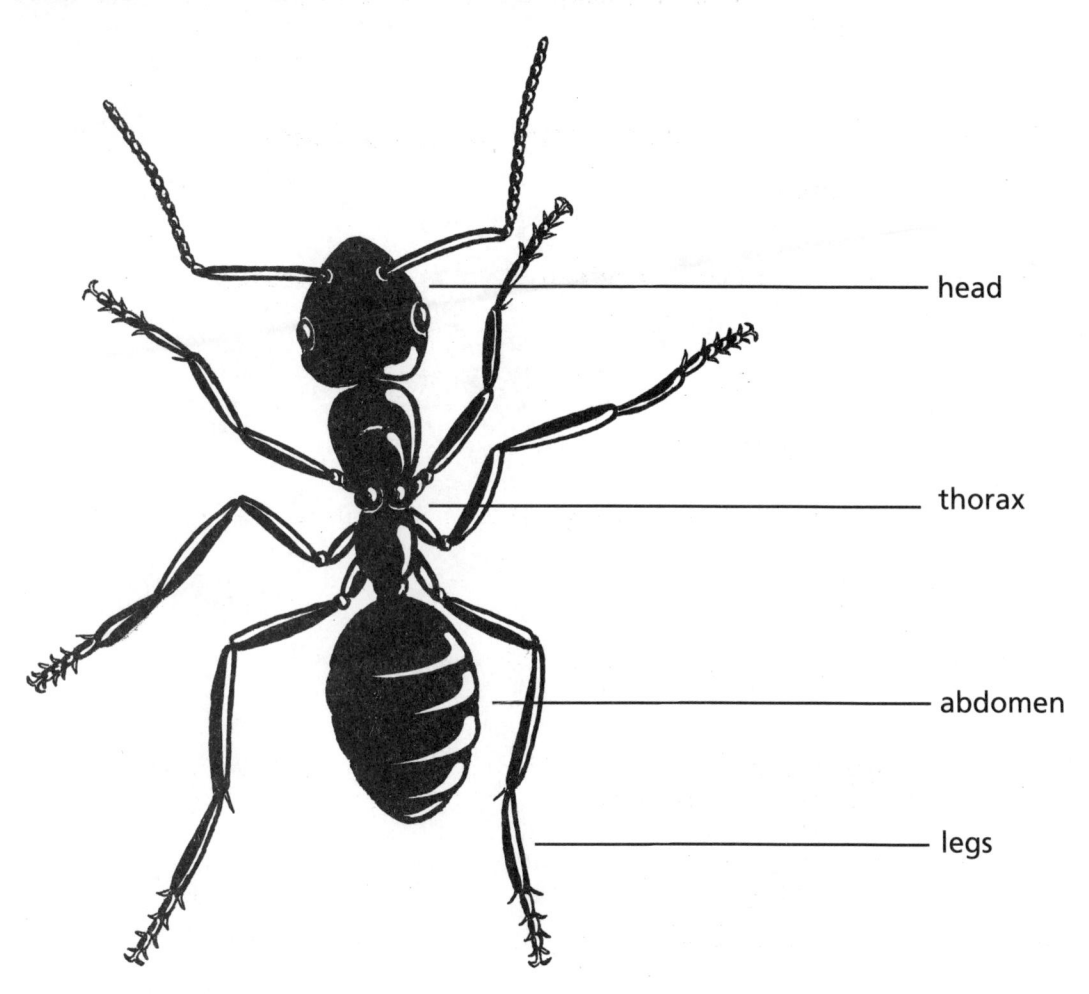

— head

— thorax

— abdomen

— legs

1. Some ants have wings but most ants do not.
2. Ants have claws on the end of their legs so that they can climb well and run fast.
3. Ants' jaws are very strong and they can chew through wood and leaves.
4. Ants have two antennae on their heads which are jointed in the middle.

Ant food

Different kinds of ants eat different kinds of food. Ants are famous for liking sweet food like sugar or jam and some live on nectar from flowers.

Most ants that come into our homes will eat almost anything. Ants that live outside eat food such as caterpillars and leaves.

Army ants

Army ants move around as a big group called a colony. When this colony is on the move it is usually looking for food. The ants eat small creatures and insects that they find, but they have been known to eat animals as large as a goat!

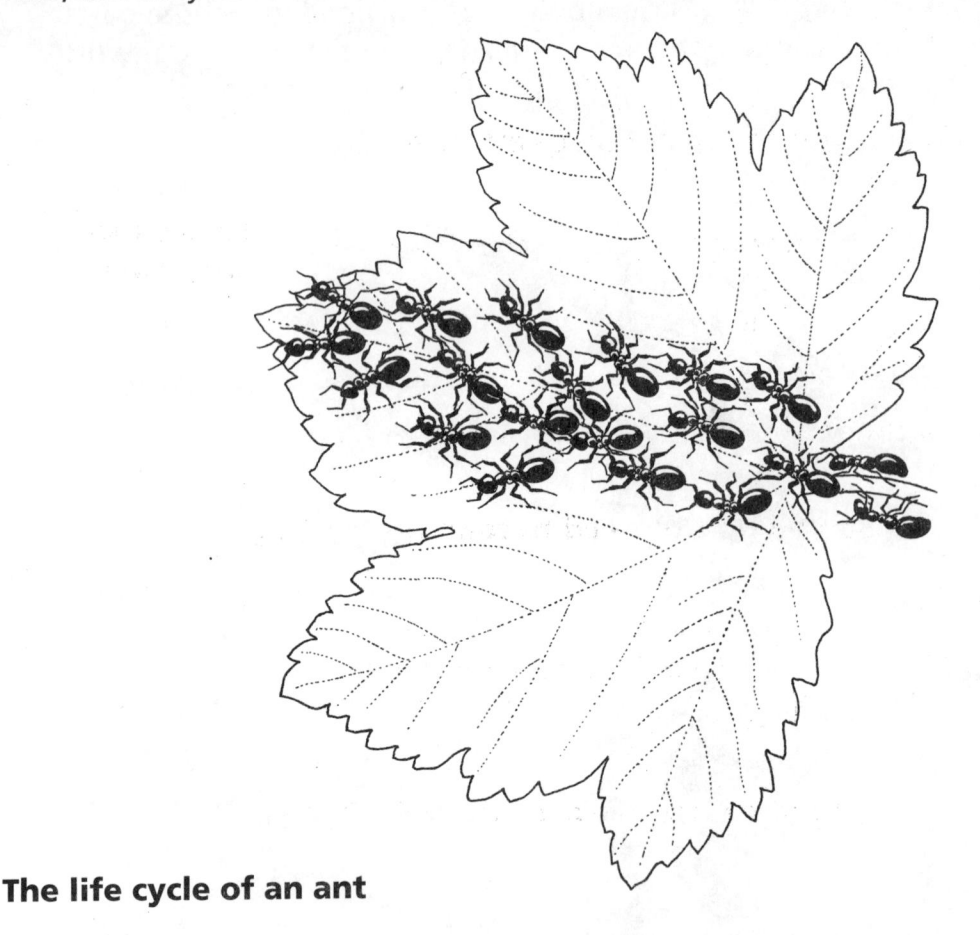

The life cycle of an ant

The ants we see running about are adult ants. They have been through four different stages by the time they are like this. These four stages are egg, larva, pupa and adult.

A queen ant is the only ant which can lay eggs.

All the eggs look the same but they develop into different kinds of ants. Most will hatch into female workers, but some develop into males or young queens. The males and young queens have wings and each young queen flies off to start a new colony of ants.

Did you know?
- Some queens and worker ants live longer than 15 years!
- In Australia some ants can be up to 2.5cm long and they have a terrible bite. In some places army ants are sometimes allowed into houses to kill other more damaging insects.

13 How many parts is an ant's body split into?

1	2	3	4
A	B	C	D

14 Which part of the body are an ant's legs attached to?

head	thorax	abdomen	thorax and abdomen
A	B	C	D

15 Why has the diagram of the ant been included?

A — so you do not need to read the writing

B — to decorate the page

C — to show the parts of the ant's body

D — because ants look interesting

16 The four points after the diagram

- A — describe the diagram.
- B — give more information about an ant's body.
- C — tell you that ants have claws on the end of their legs.
- D — tell you what ants eat.

17 Why does a colony of army ants move?

A   because small creatures may eat them

B   to fight with other ants

C   to find a new home

D   to look for something to eat

18 In the life cycle of an ant what is the next stage after being an egg?

an adult	an ant	a larva	a pupa
A	B	C	D

19 How are males and young queens different from worker ants?

A   Males and young queens cannot fly.

B   Males and young queens have wings.

C   They come from eggs which look different.

D   Males will start a new colony of ants.

20 Why do people sometimes put army ants into their homes?

A   because they may kill a goat if they are outside

B   because small creatures in the home can eat them

C   to keep them as pets

D   so they can kill insects that are causing a problem

21 The *Did you know?* box contains

advice.	facts.
A	B

fiction.	legends.
C	D

22 The writer wants us to think ants are

beautiful.	boring.
A	B

interesting.	strong.
C	D

23 Ants have several parts to their _____ .

bodys	bodeys	boddies	bodies
A	B	C	D

31

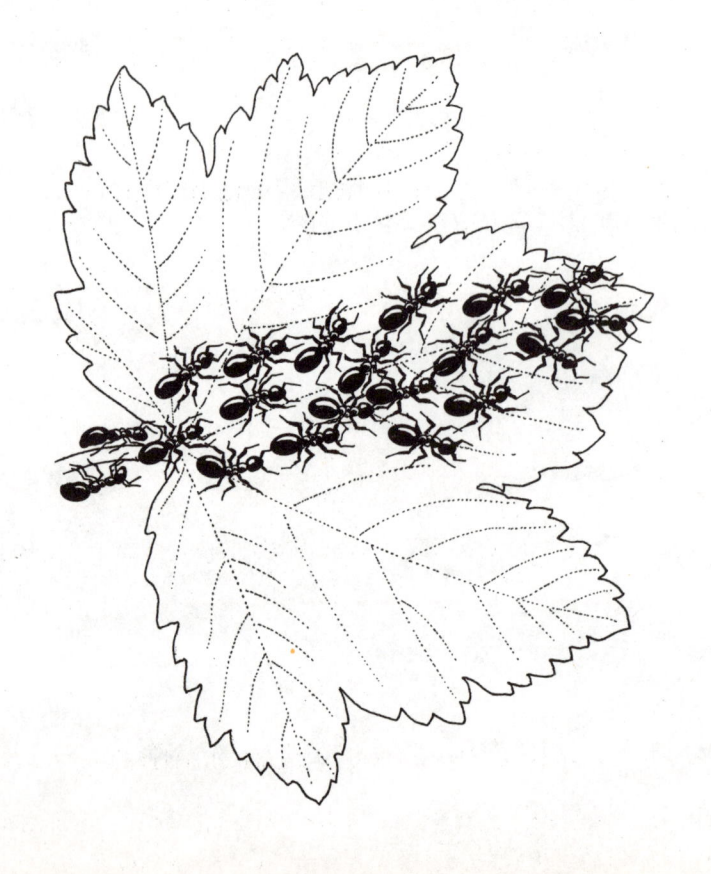

24 Ants are _____ to be the favourite food of anteaters.

suposed	supposed
A	B

serposed	sapposed
C	D

25 Not all people have a _____ for ants.

likeing	licking
A	B

liking	likking
C	D

Sandra Horn and Ken Brown
TATTYBOGLE

Old Tattybogle stood in the middle of the field. He had been there for a long, long time. He was made of sticks and sacks and the farmer's worn out clothes. His head was full of straw and cheerful thoughts.

When the wind blew, he rocked from side to side and his hat jumped up and down, but it never blew away because it was tied under his chin with good strong twine. "I like a bit of a dance!" said Tattybogle.

When it rained, the drops made a drumming noise on his hat. "Music!" said Tattybogle. Little waterfalls ran down from his floppy hat past his face. He liked that. "It's like being a statue in a fountain," said Tattybogle.

He was happy when the stars twinkled and the moon shone. Sometimes, when the nights were cold, ice-drops glimmered in the sky, high up among the stars. Tattybogle thought they were as pretty as a summerday rainbow. He was happy when the snow made a mound on the top of his hat. "It keeps my brains warm," said Tattybogle. "I feel just like a king with a silver crown."

One autumn day, the wind got up and began to blow very hard. "Good stuff!" said Tattybogle. But the wind blew harder and harder and louder. Tattybogle was rocked about so much that he felt quite dizzy. "Steady on," he said, "That's enough."

But still the wind grew stronger. It howled like a pack of wolves, tearing leaves and branches from the trees. It snatched some of Tattybogle's stuffing and scattered it all along the hedge.

"Whoops!" said Tattybogle, as the top of his hat broke off and his scarf blew away.

"Ooh, no!" he said as he spun round twice and his coat buttons were ripped off.

"Help!" he cried as the wolfwind picked him up and tossed him into the hedge.

His coat and trousers were torn away, and his stuffing was thrown into the air.

"Deary me," said Tattybogle, "all that's left of me is a stick and a few wisps of straw. I hope the farmer will find me soon and mend me."

26 Tattybogle is

- **A** a farmer.
- **B** an old man.
- **C** a puppet.
- **D** a scarecrow.

27 Tattybogle is made of

- **A** cheerful thoughts   sticks   straw
- **B** clothes   shoes   sticks   straw
- **C** new clothes   sacks   sticks   twine
- **D** old clothes   sticks   straw   sacks

28 Tattybogle's hat does not blow away because

- **A** he does not have a hat.
- **B** he has been there a long, long time.
- **C** it is fastened on with string.
- **D** it is not windy.

29 Tattybogle says, "It's like being a statue in a fountain".
What is he talking about?

people looking at him	raindrops making a drumming noise on his hat
A	**B**
the stars twinkling and the moon shining	the water pouring off his hat in the rain
C	**D**

30 Why does Tattybogle feel like 'a king with a silver crown'?

because he is important	because he has warm brains
A	**B**
because the ice drops glimmered in the sky	because the snow lay on top of his hat
C	**D**

31 When did the wind blow hard?

during the night	in the autumn
A	**B**
in the winter	when it was snowy
C	**D**

32 "Good stuff!" What do these marks " " show?

Somebody is asking a question.	Somebody is speaking.
A	**B**
Somebody is shouting.	Somebody is telling a story.
C	**D**

33 The writer says the wind was 'like a pack of wolves'.
How was it like wolves?

A because it howled

B because it snatched some of Tattybogle's stuffing

C because it tore the leaves and branches from the trees

D because it was frightening

34 In what order did bits of Tattybogle blow away?

A hat and scarf   trousers   coat buttons

B hat   coat and trousers   stuffing

C stuffing   hat and scarf   coat buttons   coat and trousers

D stuffing   scarf   hat   trousers

35 How does Tattybogle feel when the wind blows him apart?

A He is frightened because he thinks the wind is like a wolf.

B He hopes that the farmer will mend him.

C He thinks he cannot be mended.

D He is happy because he likes dancing.

36 The wolfwind *tossed* Tattybogle into the hedge.
What does the verb *tossed* tell you about how it happened?

slowly and carefully
A

gently but quickly
B

quickly and roughly
C

softly and gently
D

37 Which word best describes Tattybogle?

cheerful
A

excited
B

frightening
C

kind
D

38 Machines like ploughs and seed drills are used on _____ farms.

modern	moden
A	B

morden	modden
C	D

39 A combine harvester cuts the wheat and _____ it for storage.

prepars	prepaers
A	B

pripares	prepares
C	D

40 A baler rolls up the cut straw and ties it up into tight _____ called bales.

bundls	bundles
A	B

bundels	bundlles
C	D

David Lambert and Rachel Wright

DINOSAURS

What were dinosaurs?

Dinosaurs, or 'terrible lizards', were prehistoric reptiles. Some grew bigger than an elephant, others no larger than a cat.

Dinosaurs were not like any reptiles now living but they did have tough, scaly skin and a long tail like a lizard. They stood, walked and ran like a horse or ostrich.

There were dinosaur plant-eaters and meat-eaters. Meat-eaters mainly had sharp teeth and claws. Plant-eaters either had blunt teeth or a toothless beak and cheek teeth used for grinding leaves. Keen eyes and ears, and a good sense of smell warned dinosaurs of danger.

Dinosaurs appeared about 230 million years ago and quickly spread around the world. For 160 million years, they ruled the land. Then, mysteriously, they all died out.

Triassic times

This was the first part of the Age of Dinosaurs. At this time, all the land in the world was in one large, warm and dry supercontinent. Early dinosaurs simply walked across the world! These reptiles grew no heavier than a large dog, but from these, in the future, there would be meat-eaters as heavy as cows and plant-eaters the size of a bus.

Jurassic times

This was the middle of the Age of Dinosaurs. Long grass and tall trees grew along the side of river beds. All the land in the world had just begun drifting apart. Four-legged plant-eaters grew bony plates or spikes for protection, or evolved into the huge **sauropods**. Their enemies included **allosaurs**: large meat-eaters with huge, sharp teeth. There were smaller dinosaurs too: plant-eaters and one sort of hunter that was not much bigger than a chicken.

Cretaceous times

This period ended the Age of Dinosaurs. Flowering plants appeared and the ocean between the land widened. The weather was changing. There were more and stranger dinosaurs than ever before. North America had toothless ostrich dinosaurs, great duckbilled dinosaurs, rhinoceros-like, horned dinosaurs, and large armoured dinosaurs encased in bony plates. Tyrannosaurs, meat-eating dinosaurs which weighed as much as an elephant, killed and ate these others when they could.

GLOSSARY

allosaurs	big, meat-eating dinosaurs
Cretaceous	the last age of the dinosaurs
Jurassic	the middle age of the dinosaurs
sauropods	big, four-legged plant-eating dinosaurs
Triassic	the first age of the dinosaurs

41 What does *dinosaur* mean?

meat-eater	prehistoric
A	B

reptile	terrible lizard
C	D

42 Plant-eating dinosaurs had

a dangerous smell.	blunt teeth.
A	B

sharp beaks.	sharp teeth.
C	D

43 Dinosaurs had 'keen eyes and ears, and a good sense of smell' to

find food.	find other dinosaurs.
A	B

grind their food.	warn them of danger.
C	D

44 In the **Jurassic times**

- **A** some dinosaurs were very big and others were small.
- **B** the dinosaurs were very big.
- **C** the dinosaurs only ate plants.
- **D** the dinosaurs all had bony plates or spikes.

45 Which sentence about the **Cretaceous times** is **not** correct?

- **A** The weather was changing.
- **B** There were lots of different kinds of dinosaurs.
- **C** Tyrannosaurs ate other dinosaurs.
- **D** The oceans got smaller.

46 The passage has four subheadings. These are used to

- **A** ask questions.
- **B** make the text look nice.
- **C** give advice.
- **D** tell you what the next section is about.

41

47 What is the *Glossary* for?

- A   to explain the meaning of difficult words
- B   to make you practise reading the difficult words
- C   to show you where to find something
- D   to tell you about dinosaurs

48 Where would *dinosaur* come in the Glossary?

after allosaurs	after Cretaceous	after Jurassic	after sauropods
A	B	C	D

49 Information about dinosaurs can be found in different types of books. In which book would you **not** find this passage?

- A   in a history book
- B   in a science book
- C   in an encyclopedia
- D   in a dictionary

50 Dinosaurs _____ extinct millions of years before there were people on Earth.

became	become	bekame	becaem
A	B	C	D

Acknowledgements

First published in 2000 by Folens Limited in conjunction with OCR, Cambridge.

United Kingdom: Folens Publishers, Albert House, Apex Business Centre, Boscombe Road, Dunstable, LU5 4RL
Email: Sales@folens.com

Ireland: Folens Publishers, Greenhills Road, Tallaght, Dublin 24
Email: Info@folens.ie

Poland: JUKA, ul. Renesansowa 38, Warsaw 01-905

© 2000 Folens Limited and UCLES.

Folens books are protected by international copyright laws. All rights are reserved. The copyright of all materials in this book, except where otherwise stated, remains the property of the publisher and authors. No part of this publication may be reproduced, stored in a retrieval system, or transmitted, in any form or by any means, for whatever purpose, without the written permission of Folens Limited.

Editor: Gaynor Spry

Layout artist: Patricia Hollingsworth

Cover design: Martin Cross

Illustrations: Alan Baker, Bob Farley (Graham-Cameron Illustration), Brian Hoskin (Simon Girling Associates), Liz McIntosh (Linda Rogers Associates).

Text: Page 3: Extract from *The Tiger Child* by Joanna Troughton (Puffin, 1996) © Joanna Troughton, 1996. Page 6: Extract from *We Can Cook* by Lynne Peebles (Ladybird) copyright © Ladybird, 1979. Page 12: Extract from *Nessy* by Andrew Wright (E J Arnold & Son, 1989). Page: 17–18: Reproduced from *Usborne Book of Secret Codes* by permission of Usborne Publishing Ltd, 83–85 Saffron Hill, London EC1N 8RT. Copyright (1997 Usborne Publishing Ltd. Page 23: 'Giant' by June Crebbin. *The Dinosaur's Dinner* (Viking, 1992). 'Hurt No Living Thing' by Christina Rossetti. Page 33: Extract from *Tattybogle* by Sandra Horn and Ken Brown (Anderson Press). Page 39: Extract from *Craft Topics: Dinosaurs* by David Lambert and Rachel Wright first published in UK by Franklin Watts, a division of The Watts Publishing Group Limited, 96 Leonard Street, London EC2A 4XD.
Every effort has been made to contact copyright holders of material used in this book. If any have been overlooked, we will be pleased to make any necessary arrangements.

British Library Cataloguing in Publication Data. A catalogue record for this book is available from the British Library.

ISBN 1 84163 713–0